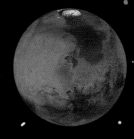

TO LISA MARIE —JR

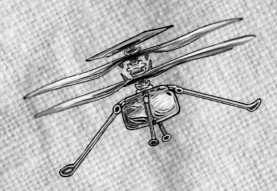

ABOUT THIS BOOK

The illustrations for this book were created by digitally combining the author's artwork with historic photographs and NASA concept art. The texture of the cloth character comes from the actual fabric swatch that Neil Armstrong took to the Moon. The photograph of this 1903 *Flyer* fabric swatch, which was carried on Apollo 11 and appears throughout this book, is by Eric Long and provided courtesy of the National Air and Space Museum. This book was edited by Jessica Anderson and designed by Ann Dwyer and Whitney Leader-Picone. The production was supervised by Lillian Sun, and the production editor was Jake Regier. The text was set in Mr Eaves Modern, and the display type is Brice.

PHOTO CREDITS

The text begins on page 6. • Photos on the following pages were provided courtesy of NASA/JPL-Caltech: endpapers (Earth, Moon, and Mars), 24 (attaching cloth to *Ingenuity*), 24 (swatch affixed to *Ingenuity*), 25 (Mars 2020 blastoff), 26 (Mars globe), 27 (*Perseverance* touchdown, main), 27 (*Perseverance* landing, inset one), 27 (*Perseverance* landing, inset two), 28 (JPL *Perseverance* mission control), 29 (*Perseverance* selfie), 30 (*Ingenuity* deployed), 30 (*Ingenuity* unfolding), 30 (*Perseverance* looking at *Ingenuity*), 31 (JPL *Ingenuity* engineers), 32 and 34 (*Ingenuity* on surface), 33 (*Ingenuity* in flight), 35 (Mars landscape), 35 (*Perseverance*), 36 (*Ingenuity* flown swatch) • Photos on the following pages were provided courtesy of NASA: title page and 20 (Earth), 16 (*Apollo* launchpad), 16–17 (Apollo 11 Personal Preference Kit), 19 (capsule, panel two), 19 (*Apollo* service module, panel three), 21 (lunar surface), 21 (lunar lander), 22 (Moon step), 23 (lunar module leaving Moon), 34 (walk on Moon) • Photos of Wright *Flyer* on pages 10–13 and 34 by Orville and/or Wilbur Wright • Photos on the following pages were provided courtesy of the National Air and Space Museum: 18 (command module interior), 19 (capsule control, panel one), 36 (Wright *Flyer* in National Air and Space Museum) • Photo of department store in Detroit, Michigan, on page 6 courtesy of the Universal History Archive/UIG via Getty Images • Photo of undergarments at the Met on page 7 courtesy of the Metropolitan Museum of Art, New York • Photo of Wright shop on pages 8 and 14 courtesy of NASA • Photo of train on page 9 courtesy of Wikimedia Commons • Photo of *Flyer* engine on page 10 by Orville Wright • Photo of Deeds Carillon in Dayton, Ohio, on page 15 by Csnoke • Photo of *Apollo* hatch on title page and pages 19–20 by Eric Long, National Air and Space Museum

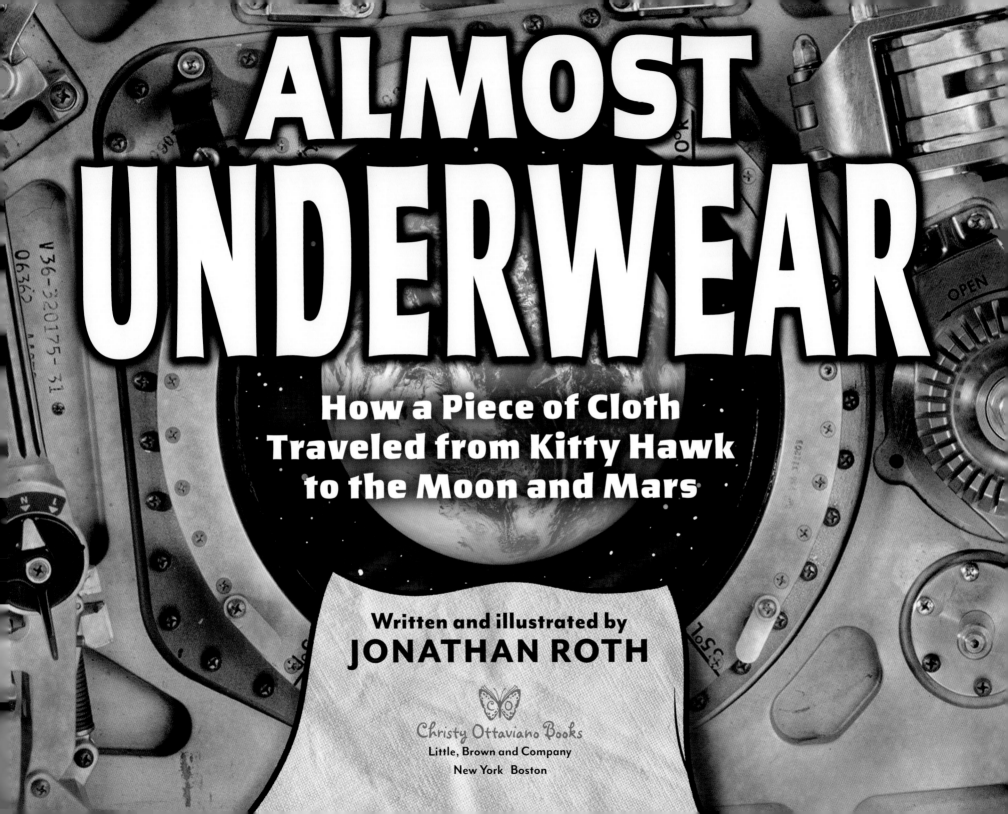

ALMOST UNDERWEAR

How a Piece of Cloth Traveled from Kitty Hawk to the Moon and Mars

Written and illustrated by
JONATHAN ROTH

Christy Ottaviano Books
Little, Brown and Company
New York Boston

Once upon a time, in a department store in Dayton, Ohio,
a roll of plain cloth waited to be transformed into underwear.

Unlike the fancier fabrics that would be cut and sewn into beautiful dresses, the tightly woven, unbleached muslin could only expect to be made into something sturdy and practical, like an undergarment.

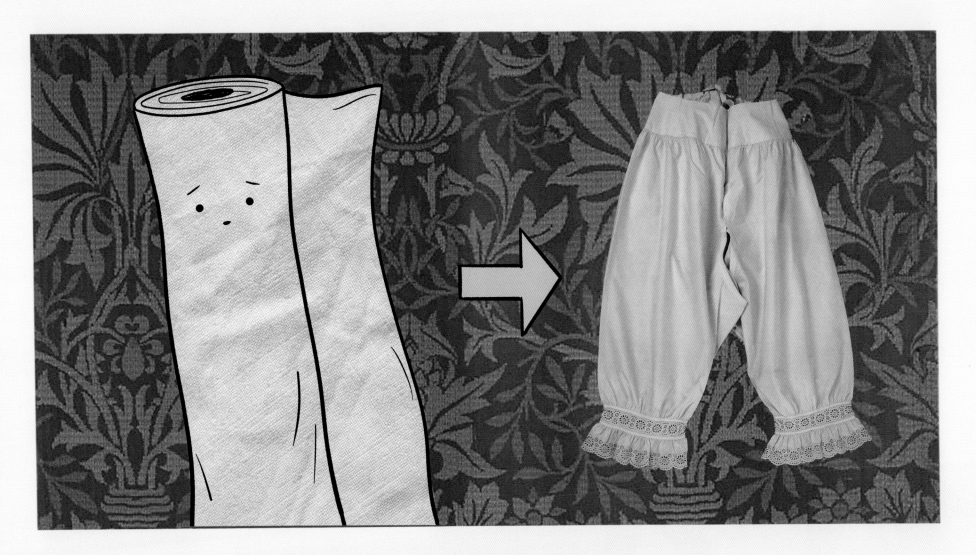

Not that underwear is bad. It just isn't destined for greatness.

The plain cloth was purchased in 1903 by Orville and Wilbur Wright, two brothers who built and repaired bicycles. They were secretly working on a new, even more fantastical way to travel.

Orville and Wilbur cut and sewed the fabric so it could fit tightly around two tapered ash-wood glider wings. The cloth worked well for gliding because it was light, flexible, and especially strong.

The brothers then packed up the wings with some other parts and traveled more than seven hundred miles by carriage, train, and ferry to a remote barrier island in the Outer Banks of North Carolina.

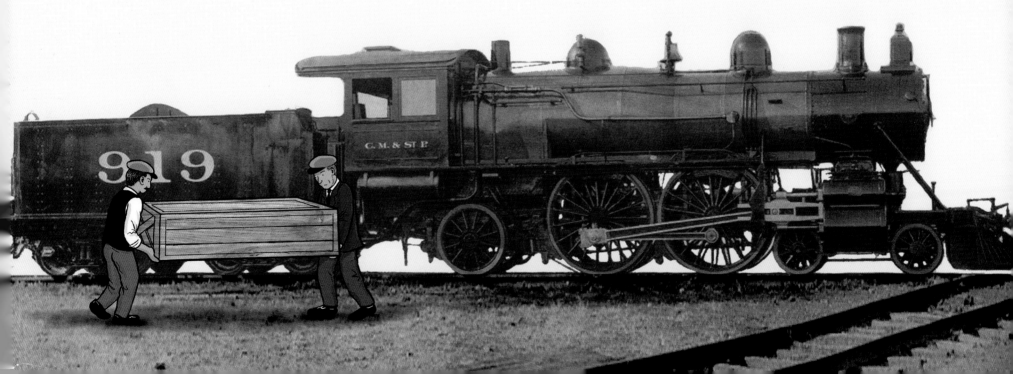

For the past three years, Orville and Wilbur had been coming to these sand dunes, just south of Kitty Hawk, to test their gliders. The winds made gliding possible, and the soft sands were safe for landing.

This time, the brothers added surprising new parts: long propellers and a bulky gas engine. How was this 605-pound contraption, the very first Wright *Flyer*, ever supposed to leave the ground?

The brothers knew that with enough speed, air pressure would build under the wide wings and push the heavy *Flyer* into the air.

On December 14, 1903, the *Flyer* took off . . . then quickly thudded into the sand. Orville and Wilbur had failed. But they learned from their mistakes, and three days later, after fixing the damaged *Flyer*, they returned to the same location.

Finally, conditions proved right. As the *Flyer* sped toward takeoff, the rushing wind under the strong cloth lifted the machine into the air. Though the flight lasted only twelve seconds over 120 feet, Orville had now piloted the first airplane in history!

The *Flyer* took off three more times—once for a record fifty-nine seconds.

Sadly, by late afternoon, a strong gust flipped and destroyed the plane. The first *Flyer* would never fly again.

The crumpled cloth was stuffed into a crate. Would it *now* be made into underwear?

Back home in Dayton, the brothers placed the *Flyer* in storage, where it gathered dust and mold for years.

But Orville never forgot about their first plane and was determined to preserve their invention for future generations.

When the Carillon Historical Park museum was being developed in Dayton in the 1940s, Orville gladly donated swatches of the original wing fabric for its collection. He died shortly after.

The historic cloth had a nice place to rest now that the adventure of a lifetime was over.

Or was it?

In 1969, Neil Armstrong was preparing for a flight of his own. He was allowed to pack only a few light items in a small, fireproof fiber bag.

To honor the *Flyer*'s contribution to aviation, Commander Armstrong included a swatch of the original wing fabric in his Moon gear.

KIT, PREFERENCE
P/N SEB 12100018-202
S/N 1009
NEIL

Sixty-six years after the Wright brothers' first flight, thousands of airplanes now carried millions of people around the globe. But would it ever be possible to fly beyond planet Earth?

Inside the bag, the cloth rumbled . . .

and shook . . .

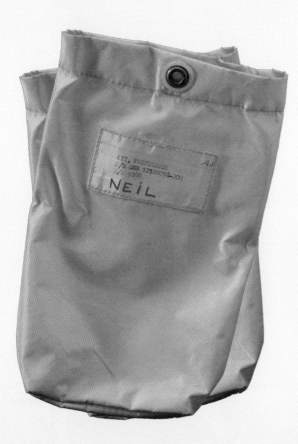

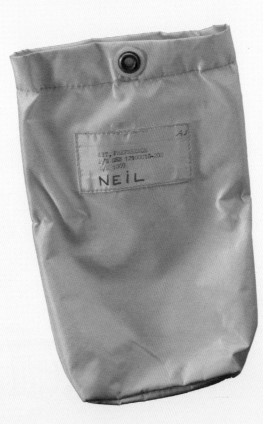

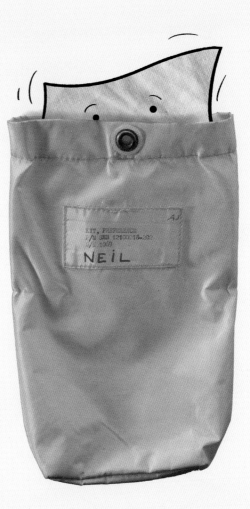

and rose with great force, until suddenly the cloth felt lighter than ever before.

Along with Armstrong and astronauts Buzz Aldrin and Michael Collins, the cloth was flying in the biggest rocket ever built! Due to the speed of the craft and its distance from Earth, the microgravity within the capsule made everything seem weightless. The cloth that had once supported the first airplane could now float.

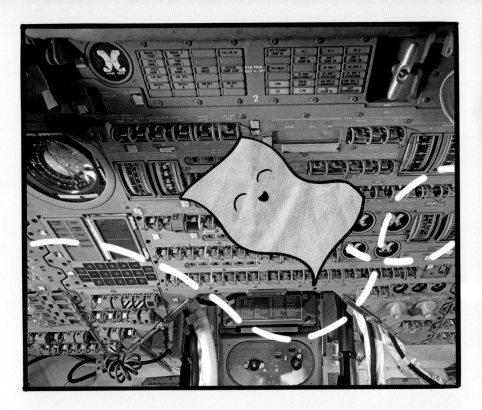

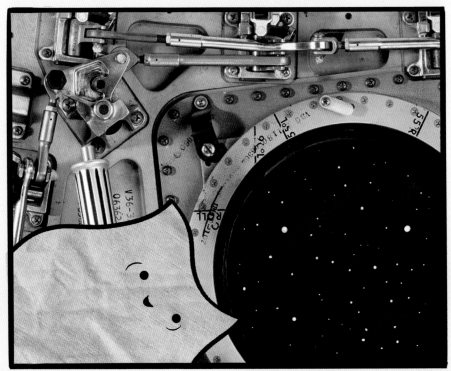

Yet the cloth's new journey had only just begun. After four days and a quarter-million miles of travel, the lunar module detached from the command module to attempt another unimaginable first: landing humans on the Moon.

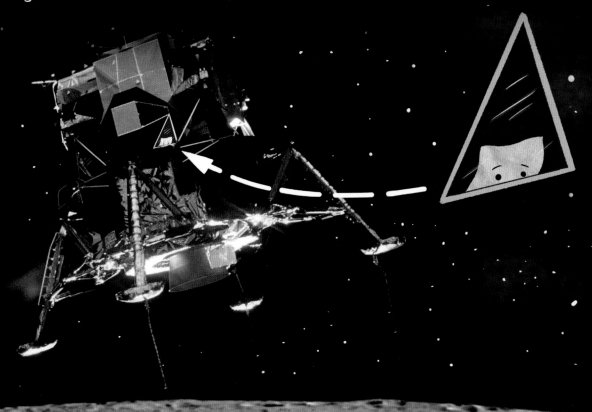

With fewer than thirty seconds of fuel left, it appeared the lander might crash. But the pilots were skilled, and they touched down on the Moon's surface in one piece.

When the hatch of the lander opened, the cloth that had once flapped in the Atlantic Ocean breeze felt only the stillness of an untouched world.

Armstrong and Aldrin performed scientific tasks on the surface of the Moon for a few hours. But as with the Wright brothers' *Flyer*, this mission mostly served to prove it could be done. After shaking the moondust out of their suits, the astronauts lifted off to meet the command module.

A piece of fabric intended to be underwear had now taken part in two of the greatest flights in human history. It was time to head home and rest for good . . .

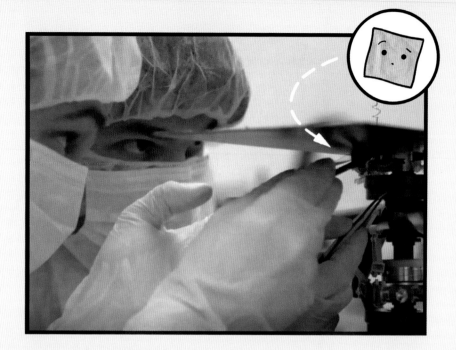

... until fifty years passed and the cloth came into action once again. A team of engineers at the Jet Propulsion Laboratory in California had just assembled a new kind of flying technology. To honor and connect with the pioneering flight from 1903, they selected and carefully sanitized a tiny piece of the old, plain cloth, then tightly secured it to a cable on the underside of their special little machine.

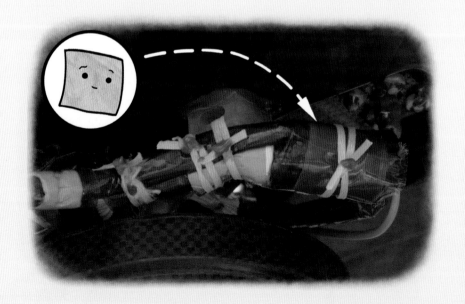

On July 30, 2020, the cloth rumbled,

and shook,

and grew lighter

once more.

Now where?

Nearly seven months and three hundred million miles later,

a spacecraft with no human passengers reached the beautiful red planet, Mars.

The landing capsule then blazed through the Martian atmosphere during what is known as the "seven minutes of terror" because of how often spacecraft perish at this stage. But the mission proved flawless, and a sky crane lowered the capsule's robotic passenger to the rocky surface below.

Back on Earth, the engineers who executed the landing could now celebrate.

Perseverance, the fifth rover to successfully reach Mars, was ready to roll. It carried many new instruments to search for signs of ancient life.

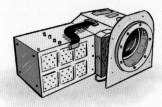

SuperCam

MEDA
weather station

MOXIE
oxygen producer
(located inside the rover, not visible here)

SHERLOC ultraviolet
spectrometer
(mounted on the rover's robotic arm, not visible here)

Mastcam-Z

PIXL X-ray spectrometer
(mounted on the rover's robotic arm, not visible here)

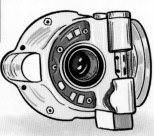

But this rover also carried a special surprise. While rovers had landed on the red planet before, no craft had ever lifted back up. Designed to test this possibility, a four-pound helicopter named *Ingenuity* was ready to go.

Instructions were sent from Earth.

The blades began to spin.

And 118 years after the first controlled flight on Earth, *Ingenuity* lifted for thirty-nine seconds, marking the very first flight on another planet.

Ingenuity flew on Mars many times. But all it ever carried was one humble little passenger who had now flown on two planets and one natural satellite.

WRIGHT *FLYER*
December 17, 1903

APOLLO 11
July 20, 1969

INGENUITY
April 19, 2021

Perhaps the most ordinary cloth can be destined for greatness after all.
In any case, it was much more fun than being made into underwear.

AUTHOR'S NOTE

In early 1903, there were no airplane parts because airplanes didn't yet exist. The earliest attempts at aviation wings consisted of wooden structures wrapped in cloth. Orville and Wilbur Wright experimented with different weaves of cloth while designing wings for their own gliders and flying machines. For their 1903 *Flyer*, they used a brand of muslin called Pride of the West, which they bought at a department store about a mile away from their bicycle shop.

Muslin is a woven cotton cloth that originated in Asia. In the early 1900s, unbleached, off-white muslin in Dayton, Ohio, was most often used to make ladies' undergarments, or underwear.

Cloth swatch just before it was attached to *Ingenuity*

The *Flyer* was designed to prove that flight technology could work. After achieving this goal, the wind-damaged plane had no further use in the air. But when it became an important historical object, the *Flyer* took on a new function: to educate and inspire. In 1916, Orville reassembled the broken plane for public display, and people have marveled at it ever since. Its permanent home is now the National Air and Space Museum in Washington, DC. While the wooden structure of the airplane on display is the original, the cloth wrapped around the wings is a replica.

In my research, I learned that what remained of the original cloth was cut into many pieces, big and small. The swatches (such as the ones Orville gave to the Carillon Historical Park) have been widely scattered, but to my delight, one of the original pieces is located in the same room of the National Air and Space Museum as the *Flyer*: the cloth artifact Neil Armstrong took to the Moon.

Though he was the first, Neil Armstrong isn't the only one to have brought *Flyer* wing cloth into space. Astronaut William Thornton took a muslin swatch aboard the space shuttle *Challenger* in 1985. John Glenn, the first American astronaut to orbit the Earth, also took a swatch on his 1998 return to space aboard the shuttle *Discovery*. Two years later, *Discovery* carried another swatch on a mission to the International Space Station.

In 2021, Bob Balaram and his team of engineers at the Jet Propulsion Laboratory decided to attach a small commemorative sample of the cloth (donated by the Carillon) to *Ingenuity*, the first experimental aircraft sent to another planet. The moment *Ingenuity* flew, I knew I wanted to write about milestones in the history of flight through the framework of older technology, threading this story back to the very moment an unsuspecting bolt of cloth was purchased by two brothers. It could have been underwear—it *should* have been underwear—and yet because of imagination, ingenuity, and a lot of perseverance, the old, plain cloth was woven into the fabric of history.

Original 1903 Wright *Flyer*, covered with a replica of the wing cloth, in the National Air and Space Museum

GLOSSARY OF *PERSEVERANCE* INSTRUMENTS

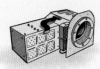

SuperCam
This device uses a camera, laser, and spectrometers to identify chemicals in Martian rocks and soils.

MEDA weather station
The Mars Environmental Dynamics Analyzer measures wind, temperature, humidity, and even the size of dust particles blowing in the wind.

MOXIE oxygen producer
The Mars Oxygen In-Situ Resource Utilization Experiment tests whether oxygen can be produced from the carbon dioxide atmosphere of Mars for the benefit of future human explorers.

Mastcam-Z
This camera mounted on the mast of the rover is used to zoom in, focus, and take 3D photos of Mars so distant objects can be analyzed in detail.

PIXL X-ray spectrometer
The Planetary Instrument for X-ray Lithochemistry measures the chemistry of Martian rocks in great detail, with the hopes of finding signs of past microbial life.

SHERLOC ultraviolet spectrometer
The Scanning Habitable Environments with Raman and Luminescence for Organics and Chemicals spectrometer on the rover's arm searches for organics and minerals that may have been affected by long-ago waters on Mars.

SELECTED BIBLIOGRAPHY

"Apollo 11." NASA. https://www.nasa.gov/mission_pages/apollo/apollo-11.html.

DeLuca, Leo. "Relic from the Wright Brothers' First Plane Flies Again on Mars." *Astronomy*, April 19, 2021. https://astronomy.com/news/2021/04/fabric-from-the-original-wright-flyer-takes-flight-on-mars.

Freedman, Russell. *The Wright Brothers: How They Invented the Airplane*. New York: Holiday House, 1991.

"Mars: 2020 Mission: Perseverance Rover." NASA. https://mars.nasa.gov/mars2020.

"Mars: Helicopter Tech Demo." NASA. https://mars.nasa.gov/technology/helicopter.

McCullough, David. *The Wright Brothers*. New York: Simon & Schuster, 2015.

Wood and Fabric, 1903 Wright Flyer, Apollo11. National Air and Space Museum. https://airandspace.si.edu/collection-objects/wood-and-fabric-1903-wright-flyer-apollo11/nasm_A19721288000.

"The Wright Brothers." National Air and Space Museum. https://airandspace.si.edu/explore/stories/wright-brothers.